The Recovery Rosary:

Reflections for

Alcoholics and Addicts

Paul Sofranko

Photographer: Rose Santuci-Sofranko

*** Photos taken at St. Joseph's Church, Oneida, NY ***

Dedication

To my beautiful wife, Rose

A thousand rose petals fall from Heaven each time you smile and say "I love you."

Table of Contents

Introduction

The Rosary is an ancient devotion prayed by Catholics. It has been around since the year 1214, when St. Dominic, as a means of converting sinners, instituted the Rosary in its present form. According to legend, St. Dominic had received it from the Blessed Virgin Mary during an Apparition in order to combat sin and heresy.

The Rosary is not about the Blessed Virgin Mary as is commonly believed by those that are unfamiliar with it. It is about Jesus. In Catholic teaching, Mary points the way to Jesus. We received Him through her: the first prophecy of Him during His life was after Simeon took Him from Mary's arms during His presentation in the Temple; His first public miracle was after her prodding (wedding feast at Cana); and she became our Mother after He gave her to his disciple John on Calvary. Mary is the path to Jesus.

It is Scriptural. The Bible is the Word of God, Jesus is the Word of God made flesh (Incarnate), therefore the Bible is about Jesus and Jesus is about the Bible.

It is also Twelve Step-friendly. The 11th Step of Alcoholics Anonymous reads:
"Sought through prayer and meditation to improve our conscious contact with God (as we understand Him), praying only for knowledge of His will for us and the power to carry it out." (from *Alcoholics*

Anonymous, 4th edition, New York: Alcoholics Anonymous World Services, Inc., 2001. Also known as "The Big Book")

You want to know God's will for you? The Bible is a good place to start looking. You want a great role model for following the will of God? His own Mother is perfect. By saying the Rosary you will be meditating on the Scriptural passages that each section of the Rosary is based on. You can nicely combine Mary's submission to God's will with direction from Sacred Scripture.

There are four groups of "Mysteries" of the Rosary. A Mystery is something Divine that we cannot fully understand with our limited human intellect.

The first are the "Joyful Mysteries." These relate to Jesus' birth. The five Joyful Mysteries are the *Annunciation.* The second Joyful Mystery is the *Visitation.* The fourth is the *Presentation of Jesus in the Temple.* And the last Joyful Mystery is the *Finding of Jesus in the Temple.*

The Luminous Mysteries, which concern the life of Jesus, are next. The first Luminous Mystery is the *Baptism of Jesus in the River Jordan* by John the Baptist. The next is the *Wedding Feast at Cana.* The third Luminous Mystery is the *Proclamation of the Kingdom of God.* The fourth is the *Transfiguration,* in which Moses and Elijah appear with Jesus on Mount Tabor. The last is the *Establishment of the Eucharist* (the Last Supper).

The next group of Mysteries are the Sorrowful, which concern the Passion of Jesus. First up is the *Agony in the Garden* of Gethsemane; the second is the *Scourging at the Pillar*. The third Sorrowful Mystery is the *Crowning with Thorns*. The fourth is the *Carrying of the Cross*. The last Sorrowful Mystery is the *Crucifixion*.

The last group of mysteries are the Glorious, which involve His post Crucifixion life and also involve Mary herself. We start with the *Resurrection*, followed by the *Ascension into Heaven*, after which is the *Descent of the Holy Spirit* (Pentecost). The fourth Glorious Mystery is the *Assumption of Mary into Heaven*. The last is Mary's *Coronation as Queen of Heaven*.

Common practice holds that the Joyful Mysteries are recited on Monday and Saturday, the Luminous on Thursday, the Sorrowful on Tuesday and Friday, and the Glorious on Wednesday and Sunday. This isn't mandatory, but in following this custom your prayers are united with all those who are also praying the Rosary that day. The Rosary is probably, after the Mass, the most common Catholic spiritual practice and devotion. It can be a means by which you can focus your sober Catholic spirituality.

After each Mystery is announced, I have written the Book, Chapter and Verse for the section of Sacred Scripture that is relevant to it. I have used the "Sacred Bible: Catholic Public Domain Version," www.sacredbible.org/catholic/index.htm a very readable modern translation. Then you would read the meditation I have written. Then please consider the meditation in light of "where you're at" in recovery. What you think about may be different from time to time, as well as over the course of the years. So I think that these are good to revisit, now and then. After that, say the prayers as per the following instructions, thinking all the while of the Scriptural passage and the meditation.

How to Pray the Rosary:

1) On the Cross/Crucifix make the "Sign of the Cross" (SOC)

2) Also on the Cross pray the "Apostles' Creed" (AC)

3) On the 1st large bead pray the "Our Father" (OF)

4) On each of the 3 small beads pray the "Hail Mary" (HM)

5) Next pray the "Glory Be to the Father" (GB)

6) On the next large bead announce the 1st Mystery; (AM) then pray the "Our Father" (OF)

7) Pray 10 "Hail Marys" (HM) on the next 10 small beads while meditating on the Mystery you just announced.

8) Next pray the "Glory Be to the Father" (GB) and the "Oh my Jesus" prayer

9) Announce the 2nd Mystery; then pray the "Our Father" (OF)

10) Repeat steps 7 and 8 then continue with the 3rd, 4th, and 5th Mysteries in the same way (repeating steps 6 – 8 for each Mystery). *If you wish to do all 20 decades, continue as above.

11) On the Medal pray the "Hail Holy Queen" (HHQ) and other ending prayers (EP)

12) On the Cross/Crucifix make the "Sign of The Cross" (SOC)

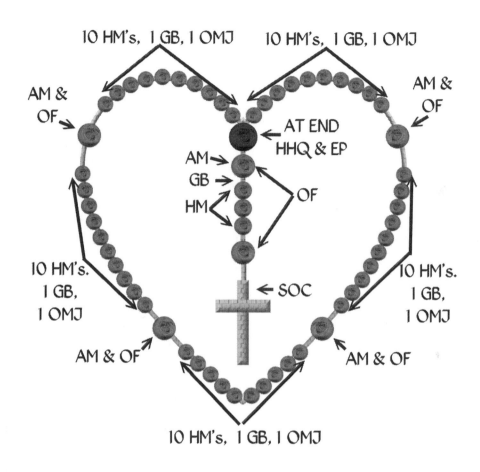

10 HM's, 1 GB, 1 OMJ   10 HM's, 1 GB, 1 OMJ

AM &
OF

AM &
OF

AT END
HHQ & EP

AM
GB
HM

OF

10 HM's.
1 GB,
1 OMJ

10 HM's.
1 GB,
1 OMJ

SOC

AM & OF

AM & OF

10 HM's, 1 GB, 1 OMJ

Prayers of The Rosary

The Sign of The Cross

In the Name of The Father, and of The Son, and of The Holy Spirit. Amen.

The Apostles' Creed

I believe in God, the Father Almighty, Creator of heaven and earth; and in Jesus Christ, His only Son, our Lord; Who was conceived by the Holy Spirit, born of the Virgin Mary, suffered under Pontius Pilate, was crucified, died, and was buried. He descended into hell; the third day He arose again from the dead. He ascended into heaven, and sits at the right hand of God, the Father Almighty; from thence He shall come to judge the living and the dead. I believe in the Holy Spirit, the Holy Catholic Church, the communion of Saints, the forgiveness of sins, the resurrection of the body and life everlasting. Amen.

Our Father

Our Father, who art in heaven, hallowed be Thy name; Thy kingdom come; Thy will be done on earth as it is in heaven. Give us this day our daily bread; and forgive us our trespasses as we forgive those who trespass against us; and lead us not into temptation; but deliver us from evil. Amen.

Hail Mary

Hail Mary, full of grace, the Lord is with thee; blessed art thou among women, and blessed is the fruit of thy womb, Jesus. Holy Mary, Mother of God, pray for us sinners, now and at the hour of our death. Amen.

Glory be to the Father

Glory be to the Father, and to the Son, and to the Holy Spirit. As it was in the beginning, is now, and ever shall be, world without end. Amen.

Oh my Jesus

"O my Jesus, forgive us our sins, save us from the fires of hell, lead all souls to Heaven, especially those who have most need of your mercy."

Hail, Holy Queen

(and other ending prayers)

HAIL, HOLY QUEEN, Mother of Mercy, our life, our sweetness and our hope! To thee do we cry, poor banished children of Eve; to thee do we send up our sighs, mourning and weeping in this valley of tears. Turn then, most gracious advocate, thine eyes of mercy toward us, and after this our exile, show unto us the blessed fruit of thy womb, Jesus. O clement, O loving, O sweet Virgin Mary!

V. Pray for us, O Holy Mother of God.
R. That we may be made worthy of the promises of Christ.

Let us pray. O GOD, whose only begotten Son, by His life, death, and resurrection, has purchased for us the rewards of eternal life, grant, we beseech Thee, that meditating upon these mysteries of the Most Holy Rosary of the Blessed Virgin Mary, we may imitate what they contain and obtain what they promise, through the same Christ Our Lord. Amen.

The First Joyful Mystery:

The Annunciation

(The Gospel according to Luke 1: 26-38)

{1:26} Then, in the sixth month, the Angel Gabriel was sent by God, to a city of Galilee named Nazareth,

{1:27} to a virgin betrothed to a man whose name was Joseph, of the house of D

avid; and the name of the virgin was Mary.

{1:28} And upon entering, the Angel said to her: "Hail, full of grace. The Lord is with you. Blessed are you among women."

{1:29} And when she had heard this, she was disturbed by his words, and she considered what kind of greeting this might be.

{1:30} And the Angel said to her: "Do not be afraid, Mary, for you have found grace with God.

{1:31} Behold, you shall conceive in your womb, and you shall bear a son, and you shall call his name: JESUS.

{1:32} He will be great, and he will be called the Son of the Most High, and the Lord God will give him the throne of David his father. And he will reign in the house of Jacob for eternity.

{1:33} And his kingdom shall have no end."

{1:34} Then Mary said to the Angel, "How shall this be done, since I do not know man?"

{1:35} And in response, the Angel said to her: "The Holy Spirit will pass over you, and the power of the Most High will overshadow you. And because of this also, the Holy One who will be born of you shall be called the Son of God.

{1:36} And behold, your cousin Elizabeth has herself also conceived a son, in her old age. And this is the sixth month for her who is called barren.

{1:37} For no word will be impossible with God."

{1:38} Then Mary said: "Behold, I am the handmaid of the Lord. Let it be done to me according to your word." And the Angel departed from her.

Many newly recovering individuals upon entering a 12 Step group discover the need to discern and follow God's will. After all, it is a part of the Third and Eleventh Steps:

Step 3: *Made a decision to turn our will and our lives over to the care of God as we understood him.*

Step 11: *Sought through prayer and meditation to improve our conscious contact with God as we understood Him, praying only for knowledge of His will for us and the power to carry that out.* (from *Alcoholics Anonymous,* 4th edition, New York: Alcoholics Anonymous World Services, Inc., 2001. Also known as "The Big Book")

How receptive are you to hearing God's will for you? Are you hoping that whatever it is, it is not something too difficult, like being called to be a missionary to some far off place? When you pray for God's will to be known to you, do you script your answer, hoping that it will influence God, as if He is unaware of what you mean? Do you reason with God, or beg Him not to do thus and so?

Mary was fully receptive to God's will. She only questioned how it was to be done, not whether it can be done or why to her. She exercised her humility as a child of God, knowing Who the Creator is and her relationship to Him, and she trusted.

An aspect of being receptive to God's will for you is trust. In trusting that He who knows you better than you know yourself, you will be guided to where you need to go and He will provide for you what you need to have. Trusting that His will for you is the reason why He placed you on this Earth.

May His will for you be done unto you, giving your acceptance upon trusting in Him.

(Now, the Our Father..., the Hail Mary..., etc., ...)

The Second Joyful Mystery:

The Visitation

(The Gospel according to Luke 1:39-45)

{1:39} And in those days, Mary, rising up, traveled quickly into the hill country, to a city of Judah.

{1:40} And she entered into the house of Zechariah, and she greeted Elizabeth.

{1:41} And it happened that, as Elizabeth heard the greeting of Mary, the infant leaped in her womb, and Elizabeth was filled with the Holy Spirit.

{1:42} And she cried out with a loud voice and said: "Blessed are you among women, and blessed is the fruit of your womb.

{1:43} And how does this concern me, so that the mother of my Lord would come to me?

{1:44} For behold, as the voice of your greeting came to my ears, the infant in my womb leaped for joy.

{1:45} And blessed are you who believed, for the things that were spoken to you by the Lord shall be accomplished."

Upon receiving the news from the Archangel Gabriel that she was to be the mother of the Messiah, and that her cousin Elizabeth was pregnant, Mary set out to tend to her at once.

Mary did not keep the stunning news that she was to be the mother of the Messiah to herself. She was also perhaps intrigued by the pregnancy of Elizabeth, who was advanced in years and previously barren. Nevertheless, her first impulse according to Scripture was to see her cousin.

She wished to serve. She, to whom the angel of the Lord declared unto her that she was to be the mother of God, *went off to serve* her cousin.

Whom do you serve? Do you share your gifts with other people, and ask for nothing in return? Do you volunteer yourself to others? Do you use any reason to excuse yourself? Even if your volunteer work is minimal, that's enough! Spend an hour a week helping an elderly neighbor with chores. Whatever it is, service work is an integral part of recovery from alcohol and addiction. It helps you to get "outside" yourself, to focus on other people rather than you. Many 12-Step Groups depend on volunteer work to open up and clean up at meetings. Service work is often lowly and unglamorous, but it is crucial. It helps you better yourself while at the same time helping others. Not that Mary needed to be in service to Elizabeth, but that makes her "Visitation" all the more meaningful. There was no need. She wanted to for the sake of it. She went "in haste".

It was an act of humility and gratitude for her, as evidenced by the following speech by Mary, referred to as the "Magnificat" prayer by the Church:

(The Gospel according to Luke 1:46-55)

{1:46} And Mary said: "My soul magnifies the Lord.

{1:47} And my spirit leaps for joy in God my Saviour.

{1:48} For he has looked with favor on the humility of his handmaid. For behold, from this time, all generations shall call me blessed.

{1:49} For he who is great has done great things for me, and holy is his name.

{1:50} And his mercy is from generation to generations for those who fear him.

{1:51} He has accomplished powerful deeds with his arm. He has scattered the arrogant in the intentions of their heart.

{1:52} He has deposed the powerful from their seat, and he has exalted the humble.

{1:53} He has filled the hungry with good things, and the rich he has

18

sent away empty.

{1:54} He has taken up his servant Israel, mindful of his mercy,

{1:55} just as he spoke to our fathers: to Abraham and to his offspring forever."

It was an act of humility and gratitude for her.

A tremendous gift and privilege was bestowed upon Mary and she was compelled to reach out to someone.

Go visit somebody.

(Now, the Our Father..., the Hail Mary..., etc., ...)

The Third Joyful Mystery:
The Nativity

(The Gospel according to Luke 2: 1-7)

{2:1} And it happened in those days that a decree went out from Caesar Augustus, so that the whole world would be enrolled.

{2:2} This was the first enrollment; it was made by the ruler of Syria, Quirinius.

19

{2:3} And all went to be declared, each one to his own city.

{2:4} Then Joseph also ascended from Galilee, from the city of Nazareth, into Judea, to the city of David, which is called Bethlehem, because he was of the house and family of David,

{2:5} in order to be declared, with Mary his espoused wife, who was with child.

{2:6} Then it happened that, while they were there, the days were completed, so that she would give birth.

{2:7} And she brought forth her firstborn son. And she wrapped him in swaddling clothes and laid him in a manger, because there was no room for them at the inn.

We all have a job to do, a mission to accomplish. There is a reason why we were put upon this Earth. We quite often put ourselves in the way of getting it done, based on the false premise that we're too good, or not good enough, or it's not our job. We resist the idea of doing this or that.

Our lack of humility sometimes prevents us from making progress in our recovery. It is as if when we stop drinking we forget the pain and humiliation we endured, we put it behind us and try to move forward on our own terms. We scrimp on the Steps, we are not willing to "work the program" (whatever it may be for each of us).

We are no longer drinking to fit in to what we think that the "world" expects of us. We may have altered our relationship with the world, we no longer feel outside, looking in. Drinking helped up bridge that perceptual gap. But now that we meet the world and accept life on life's terms we now make excuses for our recovery, or for our ability to help others.

(The Letter of St. Paul's to the Philippians)

{2:6} who, though he was in the form of God, did not consider equality with God something to be seized.

{2:7} Instead, he emptied himself, taking the form of a servant, being made in the likeness of men, and accepting the state of a man.

{2:8} He humbled himself, becoming obedient even unto death, even the death of the Cross.

Our Lord did not allow His Godhood to keep Himself from the reason He was put on Earth. He could have flushed us down the proverbial toilet and started over with another species for our crimes in Genesis 3. But he didn't, despite our crime of turning our backs on Him and seek fulfillment elsewhere, thus breaking our intimate union with Him. He still descended upon us in flesh and lived among us and died for us. He paid the price for our transgressions. It wasn't "too good" or "above Him" to bring himself down to our level.

God was not above humility. If we are to be like Christ, we must adopt that attitude. Now that we are clean and sober, we must not forget where we've been, and now we must be aware of those who may be less fortunate than ourselves. This is like an extension or continuation of the lessons from the Visitation Mystery.

(Now, the Our Father..., the Hail Mary..., etc. ...)

The Fourth Joyful Mystery of the Rosary:
The Presentation of the Child Jesus in the Temple

(The Gospel according to Luke 2: 21-24)

{2:21} And after eight days were ended, so that the boy would be circumcised, his name was called JESUS, just as he was called by the Angel before he was conceived in the womb.

{2:22} And after the days of her purification were fulfilled, according to the law of Moses, they brought him to Jerusalem, in order to present him to the Lord,

{2:23} just as it is written in the law of the Lord, "For every male opening the womb shall be called holy to the Lord,"

{2:24} and in order to offer a sacrifice, according to what is said in the law of the Lord, "a pair of turtledoves or two young pigeons."

Joseph and Mary were required to do this as Mosaic Law demanded. They submitted themselves to its authority as the faithful Jews they were. This was despite the fact that they knew who Jesus was and as a result may have thought submission was unnecessary. After all, since Jesus is God, the Author of the Law, it would seem silly. However, obedience to legitimate religious authority was expected, and culturally important.

And so they submitted. Submission to any authority is difficult for us modern time humans. We feel that our conscience and our heart should be sufficient in determining what we should and can do. What authority does the Church and State have to tell us what to do? In many circumstances, they do have legitimate authority.

But in matters of Faith and Religion, determination of God's will and such, personal autonomy can be dangerous as in these realms it is hard to safely determine what is Truth. Without guidance we can be led astray by all manner of strange teaching that appeals to emotion and superficial reasoning.

The reason I started sobercatholic.com is because in my personal experience in AA, many Catholics leave the Church and drift off into non-denominational Churches or a personal spirituality that they define. It is very fulfilling and personally empowering to design your own spiritual path. It feels very good and satisfying.

Naturally, most such paths have easier demands, for when you are in charge of your own spirituality there is the tendency to pick and choose the path of least resistance and forgo real sacrifice. As long as you feel good, things are OK. As long as you refrain from drinking, you're all right.

The problem with this is that while it may be satisfying and is keeping you sober, you are also giving up too much. The difficulties of willingly submitting to legitimate Church authority is in that it challenges you. The ascent is hard, but if accepted the spiritual progression and growth that one achieves is tremendous. If you fully accept Church authority and struggle to come into communion with her teachings, the rewards of such efforts will thwart the "rewards" of those who design their own path. Possible rewards may be a heightened knowledge of God's ways and His will and methods of determining whether it is actually Him, plus a detachment to the debilitating ways of the world, and a deeper connection with the Holy Spirit.

One reason why I rarely attend AA meetings is that I saw the same people sitting in the same chairs saying the same things about the same topics that are always brought up. My last regular meeting was in August 2004. I went back occasionally in 2005 and 2006, but the calendar on the wall could have read 2002 or 2003, for all that it mattered. I later moved away from where I sobered up, and went to a few meetings in 2011 an 2012. Despite the geographic difference, I still sensed the same feeling.

Meetings are necessary for newcomers to learn the basics, they serve as a cradle for the newly sober, or those trying to become sober. But after a time you need to leave the cradle.

And so I felt that sobercatholic.com would serve a purpose for those who are newly sober, or who have been sober for a while, but who needed something more than the comfortable spirituality offered by 12-Step movements. There are scores of blogs and websites started by non-Catholic Christians and non-Christians, that offer spiritual and religious paths to assist people in sobriety. I found little specifically for Catholic Christians, emphasizing what the Faith offers for maintaining sobriety.

Jesus said that you must enter through the narrow gate:
The Gospel According to Matthew 7: 13-14;

{7:13} Enter through the narrow gate. For wide is the gate, and broad is the way, which leads to perdition, and many there are who enter through it.

{7:14} How narrow is the gate, and how straight is the way, which leads to life, and few there are who find it!

The path to eternal life is not necessarily easy. It shouldn't be, considering the rewards. And eternal life wouldn't be accessible to us anyway, were it not for Christ's sacrifice on the Cross.

Hopefully, if you visit sobercatholic.com you learn about the Catholic

Faith and how its spirituality and devotional life can assist you in maintaining your sobriety. The idea of subordinating your natural proclivities and tendencies and willfully accepting an authority guiding you in what you should do is tough. Mary and Joseph are the models of such willing acceptance. It would be good for us to follow them.

(Now, the Our Father..., the Hail Mary..., etc. ...)

The Fifth Joyful Mystery of the Rosary:
The Finding of the Child Jesus in the Temple

(The Gospel according to Luke)

{2:41} And his parents went every year to Jerusalem, at the time of the solemnity of Passover.

{2:42} And when he had become twelve years old, they ascended to Jerusalem, according to the custom of the feast day.

{2:43} And having completed the days, when they returned, the boy Jesus remained in Jerusalem. And his parents did not realize this.

{2:44} But, supposing that he was in the company, they went a day's journey, seeking him among their relatives and acquaintances.

{2:45} And not finding him, they returned to Jerusalem, seeking him.

{2:46} And it happened that, after three days, they found him in the temple, sitting in the midst of the doctors, listening to them and questioning them.

{2:47} But all who listened to him were astonished over his prudence and his responses.

{2:48} And upon seeing him, they wondered. And his mother said to him: "Son, why have you acted this way toward us? Behold, your father and I were seeking you in sorrow."

{2:49} And he said to them: "How is it that you were seeking me? For did you not know that it is necessary for me to be in these things which are of my Father?"

{2:50} And they did not understand the word that he spoke to them.

{2:51} And he descended with them and went to Nazareth. And he was subordinate to them. And his mother kept all these words in her heart.

{2:52} And Jesus advanced in wisdom, and in age, and in grace, with God and men.

This involves one of the more interesting stories of Jesus in the New

Testament, that of Joseph and Mary losing Jesus and not finding Him for a few days. Apparently when Jesus was twelve, Mary and her husband Joseph lost track of Him when they were celebrating Jewish Holy Days in Jerusalem. He was missing for two days before they noticed. ("Joseph, do you know where Jesus is? "Um, I thought He was with you!" "No, I thought He was with *you!*" Oy, vey!!!) Anyway, they went looking for Him and found Him in the Temple, speaking with the scribes and other teachers of the Law.

This story is also among the most human, especially with regard to Jesus' parents. They are rightfully held up by the Church as ideal parents, the "Holy Family," and here they lost their child in a major metropolitan area. So in here lies hope for any parents. Even the Holy Family can mess up. But that isn't the point of this. (Well, maybe not the main point.)

Although Jesus strayed away from His family to do His Father's business, many of us strayed away from our families because of our alcoholism or addiction. Many of us stayed away for years and not just three days.

And family reunions may not have been happy, as the Holy Family's was (although reunions may have been as perplexing). Families split up. Alcoholism and addiction causes a rift and the addict goes away. Or the family tries to keep the addict in tow and controls them in hopes of "curing" or controlling the addiction. This never works and the family usually discovers Al-Anon, or its equivalent in other 12-Step movements, and learns how to cope with the addict.

Reunions can happen. Eventually (hopefully) the alcoholic realizes the need to stop drinking and drugging. They may find their way back into their family's graces, and spend a great deal of time earning back the trust that was squandered. Jesus was doing His Father's business in the Temple. His parent's didn't understand this, but apparently they accepted that. Peace was restored, they all went back home to Nazareth and Jesus never went delinquent again. He grew in wisdom and remained obedient to Mary and Joseph.

But Mary kept all these things in her heart. It was a traumatic experience despite its happy resolution, and maybe that was one of the things that she kept pondering in her heart long afterward.

Bad experiences, to whatever degree they are awful, are best never forgotten. They happen for a reason. The emotional trauma can and should be dealt with and discarded, but the experience itself should be kept a part of you and pondered for its value.

The trauma of addiction and its consequences can serve a purpose. Yes, it would be wonderful if such a purpose needn't occur. But it can sensitize you to the sufferings and trials of others. Too many of us are indifferent to the pain of other people. Not to say that addiction happens for this reason, but it is something that I learned from my own. There are probably a host of reasons that individuals can discern from their own addictions. Ponder in your own heart what value you can derive from the pain and suffering you've endured from your own hard and difficult path, or that of a loved one.

Burying the whole affair loses whatever value that can be gained. The whole experience is lost and to what end? History that is ignored often happens again.

When you find Jesus in the Temple, when you recover what you've lost, cherish and ponder it. Take it into your heart and keep it there as Mary did.

My thanks to Rose (my wife and photographer for this and some other books) for suggesting this idea.

(Now, the Our Father..., the Hail Mary..., etc. ...)

The Luminous Mysteries of the Holy Rosary

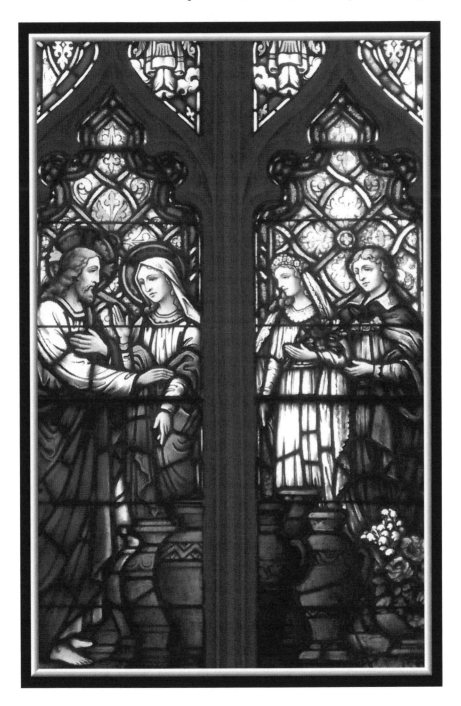

The First Luminous Mystery:

The Baptism in the River Jordan

(The Gospel according to Matthew 3: 13-17)

{3:13} Then Jesus came from Galilee, to John at the Jordan, in order to be baptized by him.

{3:14} But John refused him, saying, "I ought to be baptized by you, and yet you come to me?"

{3:15} And responding, Jesus said to him: "Permit this for now. For in this way it is fitting for us to fulfill all justice." Then he allowed him.

{3:16} And Jesus, having been baptized, ascended from the water immediately, and behold, the heavens were opened to him. And he saw the Spirit of God descending like a dove, and alighting on him.

{3:17} And behold, there was a voice from heaven, saying: "This is my beloved Son, in whom I am well pleased."

You can assume that Jesus should not need to have been baptized, as He is God, and John the Baptist did so as well. But Jesus insisted that it be done to fulfill the requirements to begin His sacramental ministry on Earth and to be proclaimed the Son of God. It was also a humble acknowledgment of His own submission as the God-become-Man to God the Father.

It heralded the start of His new life, the beginning of His mission.

We, as ones who previously were in the grip of an addiction, have embarked upon a new life. While we do not need to be baptized to cleanse us from our alcoholic past, Baptism is the mother of all the sacraments, the one we need to have in order to receive the rest, and it is through the sacraments that we can be healed of our afflictions.

The Sacraments are instruments by which God bestows upon us His many gifts and blessings, and by which we are also healed.

Jesus' receiving Baptism from John signifies this inasmuch as through that action His divinity was proclaimed. And it is through our own Baptism by which we join with Jesus and become a part of His Mystical Body (the community of all Christians, living and dead).

This is important for us Catholic Christians to understand, but it is also very useful for us struggling with alcoholism and sobriety. Everyone is ill in some way, but for those of us who suffer from an addiction, we also have this "hole in our soul" that needs filling. There was this deep spiritual emptiness within us that seemed to only be satisfied by our addiction.

This hole in our soul still needs filling after we stop our drinking.

Living a sober life (that is, having replaced alcohol with something else as a coping mechanism) gives us the sustenance we need to fill in that hole. However, as Catholics we have something more than just a method for living soberly, we have access to the Sacraments.

Participating in the sacramental life of the Church helps us to heal our brokenness and gets us closer to God.

The sacramental life is attending and participating in the Mass and receiving the Eucharist, going to frequent Confession, and living out our baptismal calling that was strengthened by the full indwelling of the Holy Spirit within us when we received our Confirmation (our own personal Pentecost).

This is a powerful aid in our ongoing recovery from alcoholism. By receiving Communion we are receiving the Real Presence of Jesus in our body. Not a symbol, but His Body, Blood, Soul and Divinity, the Real Thing. Read the Gospel of John, Chapter 6. (See also "For further information" at the end of the book.) He wasn't speaking symbolically, otherwise He would have corrected the assumptions that the "grumbling" Jews and disciples who had found His teaching hard. One of Jesus' favorite things to do was to cure people. By receiving Him in Holy Communion He is there, physically present, and ready to heal. Ask, and the healing will begin.

Confession is the other great healing sacrament. Utilizing sacramental confession frees you from your sins, removes them from your soul, and is profoundly healing psychologically. People who don't know any better refer to Confession as being responsible for "Catholic guilt". The opposite happens. If you truly believe in the sacrament, your guilt is removed. How would you feel if all guilt from your alcoholic life was removed? Your culpability and responsibility for your actions remain, but you are liberated from the sin.

The sacraments are the chief reason why I feel that Catholicism should be your primary tool in sober living.

Participate in the life of the Church. Life begets life. Talk to a priest if you need to.

Your healing has only begun!

(Now, the Our Father..., the Hail Mary..., etc. ...)

The Second Luminous Mystery of the Rosary:
The Wedding Feast at Cana

(The Gospel according to John 2: 1-11)

{2:1} And on the third day, a wedding was held in Cana of Galilee, and the mother of Jesus was there.

{2:2} Now Jesus was also invited to the wedding, with his disciples.

{2:3} And when the wine was failing, the mother of Jesus said to him, "They have no wine."

{2:4} And Jesus said to her: "What is that to me and to you, woman? My hour has not yet arrived."

{2:5} His mother said to the servants, "Do whatever he tells you."

{2:6} Now in that place, there were six stone water jars, for the purification ritual of the Jews, containing
two or three measures each.

{2:7} Jesus said to them, "Fill the water jars with water." And they filled them to the very top.

{2:8} And Jesus said to them, "Now draw from it, and carry it to the chief steward of the feast." And they took it to him.

{2:9} Then, when the chief steward had tasted the water made into wine, since he did not know where it was from, for only the servants who had drawn the water knew, the chief steward called the groom,

{2:10} and he said to him: "Every man offers the good wine first, and then, when they have become inebriated, he offers what is worse. But you

have kept the good wine until now."

{2:11} This was the beginning of the signs that Jesus accomplished in Cana of Galilee, and it manifested his glory, and his disciples believed in him.

This was Jesus' first miracle in His public life. There are several points to ponder and meditate upon that are important for sober Catholic alcoholics, namely:

This, His first miracle recorded in Scripture, was done at the request of His Mother. That in an of itself may not seem like much, but it is a part of Catholic teaching concerning Mary that states she is a co-mediator. In other words, she serves as a mediator between us and Jesus. Much like an airplane has a pilot and co-pilot, the co-pilot isn't absolutely necessary but it's nice to know that the passengers have the extra person up front for their safety. Yes, one can use just the pilot, but we humans, especially those of us staying away from alcohol and drugs are a sick lot and the extra help is useful.

We received Jesus at His birth through Mary; Simeon in the Temple (Fourth Joyful Mystery) received Jesus in his arms from Mary; the miracle at the wedding feast at Cana was initiated at Mary's request; Mary could be considered to have been His first disciple (she kept pondering things in her heart). What is a disciple supposed to do, but ponder the teachings of the Master in their hearts? Upon the Cross Jesus gave Mary to us, symbolically through the Apostle John; after His death Mary was the first to receive Him in her arms.

Through Mary to Jesus. He is our Mediator with the Father, she is the co-mediator for us with Jesus, should we wish to avail ourselves of her. And the Rosary is the best way for us to avail ourselves of her mediatrix services. And the fact that this devotion to Mary known as the Rosary focuses on *Jesus* is proof enough that devotion to Mary, through her role as co-mediator, points the way to Jesus. Jesus saves, Mary helps.

Next, He changed water (the symbol of Baptism) into wine (the symbol of His Blood and its redemptive value). This has special meaning for us in its Eucharistic nature. This, then, is a precursor to the sacraments that are the sign of grace that God grants us and in many instances heals us. These are additional important symbolisms for us alcoholics. Wine as a symbol of everlasting life, when it could mean our death if abused.

Then, we are informed towards the end of the account that this miracle was the cause of the beginning of the disciple's belief. We can work this into our own experience as sober alcoholics inasmuch as this extraordinary event took place and it caused a fundamental shift in the disciple's thinking of Jesus. They were His disciples, but, as has been demonstrated by their actions throughout the Gospels prior to Pentecost, their faith or belief in Him was problematic. They needed constant signs and indications. Prior to this episode they might have regarded Him as a great Teacher and worthy of following, maybe the leader Israel needed to expel the Romans, but a Divine Messiah? Perhaps not.

Our own conversion started when we were confronted by something that connected us to God. Perhaps it was at our alcoholic bottom, when we decided that not drinking may be better than drinking. Or maybe later on when we had achieved some measure of sobriety and found 12 Step spirituality to be insufficient. We went to Mass and heard a sermon that "spoke to us", or read some Catholic literature that got us to thinking that here lies something we need. It varies from alcoholic to alcoholic, but basically something happened that made us come to believe.

Lastly, this miracle, again – His first – was performed at a wedding. This underscores the importance that God holds for marriage, which has been made into a Sacrament by Jesus.

Although as I stated in the last paragraph that marriage is highlighted in this miracle, based on my observations of recently sober or still struggling people, either around AA meetings or halfway house residents out on privilege, is that their attitudes towards sex and relationships suffers mightily from the warped thinking that addiction causes. There is quite often a casual attitude towards sex, that it is a prize or symbol of their newly won sobriety rather than a sacred gift from God to be shared only exclusively between two people in the lifelong bond of marriage. Worse, those from rehab places out on privilege who access the Internet through public computer terminals may use their time online viewing porn, or other less-than-wholesome dating sites. This reflects a sad objectification of people, that they are there solely for personal sexual pleasure and their dignity as individual persons is disregarded.

Anyway, a number of things to meditate on.

(Now, the Our Father..., the Hail Mary..., etc. ...)

The Third Luminous Mystery of the Rosary:
The Proclamation of the Kingdom

(The Gospel according to Mark 1:14-15)

{1:14} Then, after John was handed over, Jesus went into Galilee, preaching the Gospel of the kingdom of God,

{1:15} and saying: "For the time has been fulfilled and the kingdom of God has drawn near. Repent and believe in the Gospel."

Repentance is key in receiving the kingdom of God. If the world is to be converted from its ways to ways in accord with God's will, we must start with ourselves. Once we repent, that is to have an interior change of heart and turn away from sin, then we can begin to bring about the positive steps needed to change the world and to establish lasting peace amongst peoples. Peace begins within ourselves, a peace that is nurtured and sustained through prayer, reception of the sacraments and a willful listening to the still, small voice that speaks of God's will within us.

Prayer is essential in our recovery. Prayer helps us connect with God. Start with this, the Lord's Prayer (otherwise known as the "Our Father"):

(The Gospel according to Matthew 6: 9-14)

{6:9} Therefore, you shall pray in this way: Our Father, who is in heaven: May your name be kept holy.

{6:10} May your kingdom come. May your will be done, as in heaven, so also on earth.

{6:11} Give us this day our life-sustaining bread.

{6:12} And forgive us our debts, as we also forgive our debtors.

{6:13} And lead us not into temptation. But free us from evil. Amen.

{6:14} For if you will forgive men their sins, your heavenly Father also will forgive you your offenses.

A bumper sticker I saw and almost bought says: "Prayer changes stuff." This is true.

Start by using prayer to make the needed changes within you. And stuff will be changed.

(Now, the Our Father..., the Hail Mary..., etc. ...)

41

The Fourth Luminous Mystery of the Rosary:

The Transfiguration

(The Gospel according to Matthew 17: 1-9)

{17:1} And after six days, Jesus took Peter and James and his brother John, and he led them onto a lofty mountain separately.

{17:2} And he was transfigured before them. And his face shined brightly like the sun. And his garments were made white like snow.

{17:3} And behold, there appeared to them Moses and Elijah, speaking with him.

{17:4} And Peter responded by saying to Jesus: "Lord, it is good for us to be here. If you are willing, let us make three tabernacles here, one for you, one for Moses, and one for Elijah."

{17:5} And while he was still speaking, behold, a shining cloud overshadowed them. And behold, there was a voice from the cloud, saying: "This is my beloved Son, with whom I am well pleased. Listen to him."

{17:6} And the disciples, hearing this, fell prone on their face, and they were very afraid.

{17:7} And Jesus drew near and touched them. And he said to them, "Rise up and do not be afraid."

{17:8} And lifting up their eyes, they saw no one, except Jesus alone.

{17:9} And as they were descending from the mountain, Jesus instructed them, saying, "Tell no one about the vision, until the Son of man has risen from the dead."

Jesus appeared to these three disciples of His to give them a glimpse of His heavenly glory. The appearance of Moses and Elijah with Him is to apparently bestow an Old Testament "endorsement" of Jesus as the Messiah. The authentic interpretation of what Moses and Elijah were telling Jesus was that He was being counseled on what exactly would befall Him during His upcoming trial, crucifixion and death.

What this Mystery of the Rosary means to us praying it is "spiritual courage". Not that Jesus needed much courage to face what was going to happen to Him, but that His followers needed to know that He was no ordinary human being. That despite His warning to the disciples as to what sort of death He would face, He would come through and fulfill the reason He came to us.

We all need spiritual courage. We sober alcoholics and addicts need the reassurance that despite what we are going through, we will emerge triumphant if we rely on Jesus to carry us through. "This, too, shall pass."

We have suffered in the past and have gotten through it. Yet many times in subsequent sufferings we forget this. How many times will Jesus help us get through whatever trials and troubles we experience? The answer: every single one if we trust in Him. People may fail us, deceive us and string us along, Jesus never will. Not His nature. Trust in Him, He will never fail.

Focus on this Mystery when you are experiencing trying times. Be transfigured.

(Now, the Our Father..., the Hail Mary..., etc. ...)

The Fifth Luminous Mystery of the Rosary:

The Institution of the Eucharist

(From the Gospel according to Mark 14: 22-25;)

{14:22} And while eating with them, Jesus took bread. And blessing it, he broke it and gave it to them, and he said: "Take. This is my body."

{14:23} And having taken the chalice, giving thanks, he gave it to them. And they all drank from it.

{14:24} And he said to them: "This is my blood of the new covenant, which shall be shed for many.

{14:25} Amen I say to you, that I will no longer drink from this fruit of the vine, until that day when I will drink it new in the kingdom of God."

This final Luminous Mystery is about when Jesus established the Eucharist during the Last Supper. The Eucharist is the Body, Blood, Soul and Divinity of Jesus, truly and really present in the Eucharist. Jesus comes to you again and again each time you receive Holy Communion at Mass. The Last Supper is celebrated at each Mass. When you attend the Catholic Mass, it is as if you are at the Last Supper and then also at the foot of the Cross when He died. This is something of profound importance to us Catholic Christians, but also especially for us broken by addiction and alcoholism.

Jesus heals. The same wandering Jewish preacher who healed the lepers and the blind and the crippled is right there in the Eucharist. Ask Him to heal you, whether it is of your addiction or of something else, ask Him. Your healing will begin. It may not be a miraculous instantaneous healing, it must happen in God's time, but the process and journey starts right away. Why did I say "journey"? Because for those of us who don't receive an immediate, miraculous healing, the way to being healed is a journey, one that teaches us many things: about God's will and its role in our lives, about patience and humility.

Go to Mass. It is the highest form of prayer in the Catholic Church, the summit of the Faith and the center of Catholic spirituality.

(Now, the Our Father..., the Hail Mary..., etc. ...)

The Sorrowful Mysteries of the Holy Rosary

The First Sorrowful Mystery:

The Agony in the Garden

(The Gospel according to Matthew 26:36-45)

{26:36} Then Jesus went with them to a garden, which is called Gethsemani. And he said to his disciples, "Sit down here, while I go there and pray."

{26:37} And taking with him Peter and the two sons of Zebedee, he began to be sorrowful and saddened.

{26:38} Then he said to them: "My soul is sorrowful, even unto death. Stay here and keep vigil with me."

{26:39} And continuing on a little further, he fell prostrate on his face, praying and saying: "My Father, if it is possible, let this chalice pass away from me. Yet truly, let it not be as I will, but as you will."

{26:40} And he approached his disciples and found them sleeping. And he said to Peter: "So, were you not able to keep vigil with me for one hour?

{26:41} Be vigilant and pray, so that you may not enter into temptation. Indeed, the spirit is willing, but the flesh is weak."

{26:42} Again, a second time, he went and prayed, saying, "My Father, if this chalice cannot pass away, unless I drink it, let your will be done."

{26:43} And again, he went and found them sleeping, for their eyes were heavy.

{26:44} And leaving them behind, again he went and prayed for the third time, saying the same words.

{26:45} Then he approached his disciples and said to them: "Sleep now and rest. Behold, the hour has drawn near, and the Son of man will be delivered into the hands of sinners.

This is the beginning of the end. Christ is about to be identified by His betrayer, Judas, and subsequently led off to be tried and crucified. First, He prays about it.

And this astonishes me: He, *Jesus,* is feeling *distress.* Jesus, the Son of God, is "sorrowful even unto death."

Imagine that. He is aware of what is to happen to Him soon, and is aware of the suffering He is to endure. He still seeks out His Father, seeks out some comfort or consolation about what is to happen. He seeks release from the inevitable.

Despite all this, He submits to His Father's will. Jesus does not implore for His own will to be done and to be delivered from His suffering. Instead He states a willingness to follow His Father's will. How willing are we to submit to following God's will? Even when it is painful? Our natural tendencies would be to shy away from it, hope God picks someone else and go along our own easier path.

How often are *you* the "Someone Else" in "It's Someone Else's Problem" or "It's Someone Else's Job?" As I and others better than me have stated before, it isn't easy being a Christian. The very name Christian means "follower of Christ." We do as He did. We accept suffering as part of the path to our salvation. We seek the Father's will as He did. Cynics might say that it was easy for Jesus as He is God, but as followers of Christ and as adopted children of God we can draw upon the strength of His divinity. Being a Christian isn't about accepting Jesus Christ as your Lord and Savior and then having a life that's all butterflies and buttercups. It's humbling yourself to the painful reality that there is a God and you are not Him and that you may have to live according to ways that are contrary to your natural tendencies, political and social beliefs and other peer-pressure situations. Ultimately you realize that this is a sort of natural freedom, living by Gods' will and not your own. Your own will is influenced and corrupted by the World, which is usually in opposition to God's will. (Hence the existence of evil.)

You undergo trials, tribulations and sufferings. Pray about them. Do not seek to avoid them, but don't feel bad about wanting to. When you pray about them ask God for His will in enduring the pain. Why is He allowing or permitting this to happen? Not as in "Why is this happening to me and not to Someone Else?", but rather, "How is this necessary for my salvation?"; "How will enduring this aid in my spiritual development and become closer to God?"

Ponder these when you enter into your own Garden of Gethsemane and begin your agony.

(Now, the Our Father..., the Hail Mary..., etc. ...)

The Second Sorrowful Mystery:
The Scourging at the Pillar

(From the Gospel according to John 19:1)

{19:1} Therefore, Pilate then took Jesus into custody and scourged him.

Scourging means whipped. The flesh is punished and severe pain and agony is the result.

Giving up our addictive substance is our own "scourging at the pillar." We have given up our addictions and we suffer from being deprived of them. This decade of the Rosary is therefore an especially pertinent one in our struggles. Our addictive self tries to rise again, and as we battle against the flesh, we are tempted in our journey to relapse.

It is as if we are undergoing our own personal season of Lent, a time when we have to "give up" something (or maybe do something outside your comfort zone) or otherwise engage in some form of mortification.

While not endorsing the painful and strange physical mortifications that Christians undertook centuries ago for penance, some sort of mortification is necessary to experience the full spiritual benefits of any Lent and the torrent of graces offered by God.

Giving up drinking is certainly mortifying enough for a personal Lenten season. We offer up what we missed and perhaps enjoyed. And we most certainly offer up the temptations to drink again.

What do you "give up" or "do?" for Jesus?

(Now, the Our Father..., the Hail Mary..., etc. ...)

The Third Sorrowful Mystery
The Crowning of Thorns

(The Gospel according to John 19:2)

{19:2} And the soldiers, plaiting a crown of thorns, imposed it on his

head. And they put a purple garment around him.

Imagine Jesus, the King of Kings, being crowned, not with a proper one of gold and fine gems, but with a crown woven of thorns. Imagine the humiliation. Humiliation is something we alcoholics are familiar with regardless of the length of our sobriety. Jesus endured His. Quietly He accepted the shouts and jeers and abuse. Did we? Probably not. In our alcoholic state we more than likely viewed ourselves as victims of our humiliations, rather than being responsible for causing them.

It is fitting that the lesson of this mystery is focused on a targeting of the head. For it is within the confines of the mind that the disease (or whatever it is) of alcoholism takes place. It is from within the confines of the mind that how we responded to the real world determined that we drink. It is within the confines of the mind that our alcohol-inspired fantasies drove us to our behavior, and our humiliating awareness of what the real world thought of our fantastic delusions.

We awakened to our own humiliations and decided. Do we drink and die? Or do we stop drinking and maybe live? Jesus accepted His humiliation and on the third day after, He rose again, opening the path to our own eternal salvation. If we, as Christians, are to be like Him, we can do something with our own humiliations and accept them as being a part of us. They were the cause of our own resurrection. (Several years ago while I was still very early in my recovery from drinking I was watching a Mass on EWTN. A priest (Fr. Angelus Shaughnessy) gave a homily in which he said something like that "there is no humility without accepted humiliation.")

Humiliation attacks our pride. Whether the humiliation is the result of our own shortcomings or of cruelty by others, accepting it as a suffering enables us to become more humble, more Christ-like in our ways.

Accept your past. The person you were before made you the person you are today.

(Now, the Our Father..., the Hail Mary..., etc. ...)

The Fourth Sorrowful Mystery:
Jesus Carries His Cross

Excerpts from 3 Gospel accounts:
(The Gospel according to Luke 9:23)

{9:23} Then he said to everyone: "If anyone is willing to come after me: let him deny himself, and take up his cross every day, and follow me.

(The Gospel according to Luke 14:27)

{14:27} And whoever does not bear his cross and come after me, is not able to be my disciple.

(The Gospel according to John 19:16-17)

{19:16} Therefore, he then handed him over to them to be crucified. And they took Jesus and led him away.

{19:17} And carrying his own cross, he went forth to the place which is called Calvary, but in Hebrew it is called the Place of the Skull.

We all have crosses to bear. All the daily trials and troubles common to everyone, but quite often more serious issues like health and occupation.

These are the crosses that are given to us, just as Christ Himself was given a cross to bear. He did not shirk His cross, but undertook it because He knew it was needed to open Heaven for us. Without His death and resurrection, Heaven would have remained forbidden to humanity, as the consequence of the sin of Adam and Eve.

We should not shirk our crosses, for by accepting them as we Christians should as disciples of Jesus, we therefore move towards the Heaven He opened for us.

All the crosses that enter your life are there to assist you in your way to salvation. When we are given a cross to bear, it is a sign of our adoption by God as His children, for He allows the same thing to happen to us as He allowed to happen to His own Son.

Accept your cross willingly. Pray to God that you are able to discern its meaning in your life.

(Now, the Our Father..., the Hail Mary..., etc. ...)

The Fifth Sorrowful Mystery:

Jesus Dies on the Cross

(The Gospel according to Mark 15:37)

{15:37} Then Jesus, having emitted a loud cry, expired.

Jesus dies. His body succumbs to death and He departs to the abode of the Dead, where the just and righteous people who have died before Him await His coming to lead them to Heaven.

And on the third day after, He arises from the dead and to a new life.

We alcoholics who drank have been resurrected from the dead, so to speak, when we stopped drinking and learned to live without alcohol.

As Jesus was released from the confines of His human body when He died, so, too, are those released from the confines of their addiction when they begin or maintain their recovery. Our old self died, and we were resurrected. Our new lives began with hopefully a new plan for them.

His body died on the Cross. So can your addiction. Nail it to the Cross of Christ. Allow your devotion to Jesus to surpass your desire to drink (or to return to drinking). Be a Christian and willingly accept the crosses that come into your life as methods to grow closer to God. Fools blame God for the sorrows of their lives and run from Him. We Christians know better. As Jesus suffered, so must we accept our suffering. Jesus died on the Cross. His death means your freedom.

(Now, the Our Father..., the Hail Mary..., etc. ...)

The Glorious Mysteries of the Holy Rosary

The First Glorious Mystery:

The Resurrection of Jesus

(The Gospel according to Matthew 28: 1-10)

{28:1} Now on the morning of the Sabbath, when it began to grow light on the first Sabbath, Mary Magdalene and the other Mary went to see the sepulcher.

{28:2} And behold, a great earthquake occurred. For an Angel of the Lord descended from heaven, and as he approached, he rolled back the stone and sat down on it.

{28:3} Now his appearance was like lightning, and his vestment was like snow.

{28:4} Then, out of fear of him, the guards were terrified, and they became like dead men.

{28:5} Then the Angel responded by saying to the women: "Do not be afraid. For I know that you are seeking Jesus, who was crucified.

{28:6} He is not here. For he has risen, just as he said. Come and see the place where the Lord was placed.

{28:7} And then, go quickly, and tell his disciples that he has risen.

And behold, he will precede you to Galilee. There you shall see him. Lo, I have told you beforehand."

{28:8} And they went out of the tomb quickly, with fear and in great joy, running to announce it to his disciples.

{28:9} And behold, Jesus met them, saying, "Hail." But they drew near and took hold of his feet, and they adored him.

{28:10} Then Jesus said to them: "Do not be afraid. Go, announce it to my brothers, so that they may go to Galilee. There they shall see me."

If we are alcoholics and are now sober, then the we have died an alcoholic death of sorts. The alcoholic within us has died, hopefully never to appear again through our own weaknesses and lack of proper sober living.

What has occurred instead has been a "resurrection", the rebirth of the person we were supposed to be had we never taken up drinking. By some mysterious workings of God's will, we have become "wiser" through the experience of alcoholism and the subsequent recovery process. Although we have finally become that person God created us to be, through the experience of our alcoholism are far more appreciative of the "normal" life we now lead, and are perhaps far more attuned to the sufferings and faults of other people.

Creation is an ongoing process; we are never complete or whole at birth or even at early adulthood. For reasons known only to God our "creation" needed the added elements of addiction. Admit it: we alcoholics and addicts who are no longer slaves to our condition have deeper insights into human misery and suffering than most. We also better appreciate the things others take for granted. We are living out our resurrected lives as living examples of our transformation, similar to Jesus' post Resurrection appearances to His disciples. They had to see and witness to believe He was raised, as do our families and friends need to witness our new lives to believe (although doubt remains for a long time, depending on how long we drank and what we did. Trust takes a while to be earned.).

(Now, the Our Father..., the Hail Mary..., etc. ...)

The Second Glorious Mystery:
The Ascension of Jesus into Heaven

(The Gospel according to Mark 16: 19-20)

{16:19} And indeed, the Lord Jesus, after he had spoken to them, was taken up into heaven, and he sits at the right hand of God.

{16:20} Then they, setting out, preached everywhere, with the Lord cooperating and confirming the word by the accompanying signs.

61

Jesus ascended to Heaven after His Resurrection to reunite with the Father. Following the Father's will was essential to Jesus' nature. If we as Christians are to follow Christ, then we also must "ascend" to the Father as well. While we obviously cannot ascend to Heaven on our own wills, we can unite ourselves ("ascend") to the Father through prayer and meditation, through reception of the Eucharist and participating in the sacramental life of the Church.

Remember what was said in the First Joyful Mystery about God's Will:

"Many newly recovering individuals upon entering a 12 Step group discover the need to discern and follow God's will. After all, it is a part of the Third and Eleventh Steps."

Step 3: *Made a decision to turn our will and our lives over to the care of God as we understood him.*

Step 11: *Sought through prayer and meditation to improve our conscious contact with God as we understood Him, praying only for knowledge of His will for us and the power to carry that out.* (from *Alcoholics Anonymous,* 4th edition, New York: Alcoholics Anonymous World Services, Inc., 2001. Also known as "The Big Book")

The Church is Heaven on Earth, and in taking part more fully in the Church's mission we are thus doing the Father's will. We are building up the Kingdom of God. The Lord will work with us and confirm our actions through signs that accompany our work. And the Church, guided by the Holy Spirit in teaching matters of Faith and Morals, can help us discern God's Will for us.

How are you "ascending" to the Father? How are you working to build up the Kingdom of God? You may be to only "Gospel" that people see. Is Christ visible in you?

(Now, the Our Father..., the Hail Mary..., etc. ...)

The Third Glorious Mystery:
The Descent of Holy Spirit

(The Acts of the Apostles 2:1-4)

{2:1} And when the days of Pentecost were completed, they were all together in the same place.

{2:2} And suddenly, there came a sound from heaven, like that of a wind approaching violently, and it filled the entire house where they were sitting.

{2:3} And there appeared to them separate tongues, as if of fire, which settled upon each one of them.

{2:4} And they were all filled with the Holy Spirit. And they began to speak in various languages, just as the Holy Spirit bestowed eloquence to them.

The Holy Spirit is our guide. The Spirit descended to guide and assist the followers of Jesus in navigating through the traps of the World. If in humility we try prayer and meditation to discern the "still, small voice" that is the will of God speaking through the Spirit's interior promptings, we will be able to cooperate with Him who is our Father in Heaven. We will participate with Him in establishing the Kingdom of God on Earth.

Twelve Step movements always refer to a "Higher Power," some personally defined "power greater than yourself" to help guide us in our recovery. For us Catholic Christians it is clear that our Higher Power is Jesus Christ, and the Guide He left behind to teach us and instruct us in the way we should go. That Guide is the Holy Spirit.

So, how often do your rely of the Holy Spirit for guidance?

It starts with ourselves. If we seek the Holy Spirit's guidance in our daily activities then we shall better maintain our sobriety. From then on we can change the world (or just our little corner of it.)

(Now, the Our Father..., the Hail Mary..., etc. ...)

The Fourth Glorious Mystery:

The Assumption of the Blessed Virgin Mary into Heaven

This is when the Mother of God was bodily taken up into Heaven rather than suffering the corruption of death. The Eastern Orthodox Christian Churches and the Byzantine Rite Catholics refer to this as Mary's "Dormition", or "falling asleep".

Rather than dying and suffering the corruptibility of death, she was bodily assumed into Heaven. (She was free of Original Sin, being immaculately conceived, and bodily decay is a consequence of Original Sin (the Fall of Adam and Eve in Genesis Chapter 3). See "For more information" links at the end of this book.)

None of us are sinless, except for Mary. As we know all too well upon reviewing our alcoholic past and life in general, we had strayed quite often from doing the will of God, and in fact many times outright offended Him.

We Catholics have recourse to the Sacrament of Confession (also known as "Reconciliation"). We see a priest (who acts in the place of Jesus) and confess our wrongdoings and offenses against God and receive absolution and a penance. We amend our lives and struggle to live according to His will.

Mary can be our guide and model. She who was sinless can serve to be the one who will intercede for us if we only ask her. We can use the Rosary as both the weapon in our battle against sin and as the method by which we solicit her help.

(The Book of Genesis 3:16,19,20)

{3:16} To the woman, he also said: "I will multiply your labors and your conceptions. In pain shall you give birth to sons, and you shall be under your husband's power, and he shall have dominion over you."

{3:19} By the sweat of your face shall you eat bread, until you return to the earth from which you were taken. For dust you are, and unto dust you shall return."

{3:20} And Adam called the name of his wife, 'Eve,' because she was the mother of all the living.

(The Gospel according to Luke 1:26-38)

{1:26} Then, in the sixth month, the Angel Gabriel was sent by God, to a city of Galilee named Nazareth,

{1:27} to a virgin betrothed to a man whose name was Joseph, of the house of David; and the name of the virgin was Mary.

{1:28} And upon entering, the Angel said to her: "Hail, full of grace.

The Lord is with you. Blessed are you among women."

{1:29} And when she had heard this, she was disturbed by his words, and she considered what kind of greeting this might be.

{1:30} And the Angel said to her: "Do not be afraid, Mary, for you have found grace with God.

{1:31} Behold, you shall conceive in your womb, and you shall bear a son, and you shall call his name: JESUS.

{1:32} He will be great, and he will be called the Son of the Most High, and the Lord God will give him the throne of David his father. And he will reign in the house of Jacob for eternity.

{1:33} And his kingdom shall have no end."

{1:34} Then Mary said to the Angel, "How shall this be done, since I do not know man?"

{1:35} And in response, the Angel said to her: "The Holy Spirit will pass over you, and the power of the Most High will overshadow you. And because of this also, the Holy One who will be born of you shall be called the Son of God.

{1:36} And behold, your cousin Elizabeth has herself also conceived

a son, in her old age. And this is the sixth month for her who is called barren.

{1:37} For no word will be impossible with God."

{1:38} Then Mary said: "Behold, I am the handmaid of the Lord. Let it be done to me according to your word." And the Angel departed from her.

(The Book of Revelation 12:1, 5)

{12:1} And a great sign appeared in heaven: a woman clothed with the sun, and the moon was under her feet, and on her head was a crown of twelve stars. ...

{12:5} And she brought forth a male child, who was soon to rule all the nations with an iron rod. And her son was taken up to God and to his throne.

(Now, the Our Father..., the Hail Mary..., etc. ...)

The Fifth Glorious Mystery:
The Coronation of the Blessed Virgin Mary as Queen of Heaven

I was initially perplexed as to what to write about regarding this Mystery, at least as it pertains to sober Catholics. The idea of a "Queen" may be outside the frame of reference for most readers, except perhaps those living in the United Kingdom and other countries formerly a part of the British Empire. The notion of a monarch, ideally a benevolent ruler, may provide some comfort to those who see the world as chaotic as it is. I was a Political Science and International Studies major in college, and was taught that by modern times monarchs served mainly as "Heads of State", and not in any direct capacity of governing. This meant that the monarch was to serve as the example of the best that the country offered, and was above politics. Reality sometimes proves that wrong, but no matter. The idea is there. In the Blessed Virgin Mary we have our ideal monarch. Mary is our Queen to serve as our role model and guide, and intercessor for us to the Father. She is the best that our species has to offer, our only great success story.

In the Holy Rosary we can offer up to her our prayers, wants, needs and worries. She takes them all and delivers them to God. As Mary is the Daughter of God the Father, the Mother of God the Son, and the Spouse of God the Holy Spirit, what better benefactor can we have than her?

Mary followed God's will. When learning something about Jesus she always "pondered them in her heart." We can do likewise. We can read the Gospels and "ponder in our heart" what we read there. The Gospels are a guide to living, sober or otherwise.

So, pray the Rosary. Ideally daily, but if not, as often as you can. It can be a great comfort.

(The Book of Revelation 12:1)

{12:1} And a great sign appeared in heaven: a woman clothed with the sun, and the moon was under her

feet, and on her head was a crown of twelve stars. ...

(Now, the Our Father..., the Hail Mary..., etc. ...)

For further information:

"How to Say the Rosary"

http://www.newadvent.org

"Sacred Bible: Catholic Public Domain Version

http://www.sacredbible.org/catholic/index.htm

Immaculate Conception (and Mary's Assumption):

http://www.ewtn.com/faith/teachings/marya2.htm

Mary as Co-Mediator:

http://www.ewtn.com/faith/teachings/marya4.htm

The Real Presence:

http://www.ewtn.com/faith/teachings/eucha3.htm

For additional information, you may also go to http://sobercatholic.com. See the sections entitled "The Church and the Bible," "Rosary," "How to Become Catholic or Return to the Church," and "For all things Catholic..." These all contain untold riches of information on essentially anything that I have written in this book that you may have questions on. Go and explore, you'll never know what you'll find!

About the Author

Paul Sofranko sobered up on May 22, 2002. Afterwards, he decided that while a 12 Step Program may be effective and very useful for some, he needed something more. Therefore he explored the religion of his childhood and returned to the Catholic Church, from which he had been away for nearly 15 years. He's been happy with his decision ever since.

Connect with Me Online:

I blog at:

www.SoberCatholic.com

For more information about the photographer,

Rose Santuci-Sofranko, please go to:

www.Artist4God.net